EXECUTIVE SUMMARY

1. This paper is an independent analysis of the economic and social challenges facing Scotland's public services, and how the radical reform of services through innovation could help to meet some of these challenges. It argues that innovation – developing new approaches that are better at preventing and solving problems for and with citizens – is critical to making sustainable savings in public services and to ensuring a stronger, safer, healthier and more productive Scotland.

2. As has been identified by the Chief Economic Adviser and the Independent Budget Review (IBR), public spending in Scotland faces substantial reductions in real terms following the financial crisis and the deficit reduction plan set out by the Westminster Government. Estimates ahead of the Comprehensive Spending Review (due October 2010) suggest that the Scottish Government's budget will be reduced by a total of £3.7 billion by 2014-15 – the largest reduction in spending since the Second World War. Even a range of highly contentious measures considered in the IBR would produce only around three-quarters of these savings, leaving a gap of £1 billion which could only be filled by direct cuts to public services.

3. Such reductions could risk significant economic and social harm. Managing reductions in spending in a careful and considered way is especially important for Scotland. Public services represent a larger proportion of the economy than they do in the UK as a whole, hence reductions in spending have an even greater potential to harm not only individuals and communities directly, but also Scotland's economy and society generally.

4. However, a careful and considered response to spending reductions is not the same as a conservative approach. Even without needing to make savings, Scottish public services have been struggling to meet rising demand and respond to the changing needs of citizens.

5. Scotland faces some deeper social challenges than the rest of the UK. Conditions such as those associated with obesity, entrenched inequalities and high rates of re-offending have traditionally been hard to meet through largely uniform provision and are putting urgent and expensive pressures on public services. Over the next 15 years Scotland's public services will need to cope with additional demands in health, social care and justice alone amounting to more than £27 billion, due in particular to an ageing society and the prevalence of certain ill-health conditions.

6. Services need to innovate to respond more effectively and efficiently to complex social problems that cannot easily be 'fixed' by standardised provision. This paper highlights examples of innovation (including from Scotland) that demonstrate how to save money and improve outcomes by managing and reducing demand for services, through meeting people's needs more effectively and building their own capability to prevent and respond to problems. These innovations can be characterised by their distinctly local approach and how they engage the public directly in designing and delivering services. The more that this kind of innovation plays a role in reducing spending and improving outcomes, the less emphasis might need to be placed on other contentious and potentially harmful measures.

7. We propose an ambitious new way for local public services to lead the next stage of radical reform in Scotland that saves money and improves outcomes for citizens. We propose new powers and responsibilities for leading authorities and public bodies that take forward the Concordat, Single Outcome Agreements and existing frameworks. This mechanism – a 'New Community Status' – would provide greater local agency for developing new approaches in public services that are both better and cheaper. Locally led innovation would be guided and supported by national programmes of reform and reinvestment,

to progressively decommission some capacity from some existing services (such as acute care in hospitals) and shift investment to new approaches that manage and reduce demand more effectively.

8. New community status would grant more public services such as local authorities and health boards access each year to a 'rebate' equivalent to up to 1 per cent of their annual budgets in health, justice or social care, funded through disinvestment in existing demand-led services. In return, providers would have to return half of the savings they make as a result of innovation activities to central government each year, and they would have to 'repay' at least half of the rebate to central government by the end of the Spending Review period.

9. New community status would also mean an obligation to conduct a local assessment of where resources are currently spent and how effective this spending is, to develop new more appropriate measures of success, and to work in partnership with employees, the social sector, and the local community to develop and deliver new approaches. If successful, new community status could become the normal relationship between local providers and central government during the following Spending Review period (that is, post 2014-15).

CONTENTS

Part 1: The challenges facing public services in Scotland   7

Part 2: How radical reform in public services can reduce demand and improve outcomes   16

Part 3: Transforming Scotland's public services   31

Conclusion   47

Endnotes   48

NESTA in Scotland: Innovation in public services   55

PART 1: THE CHALLENGES FACING PUBLIC SERVICES IN SCOTLAND

The financial challenge

10. Public services in Scotland face substantial reductions in real terms, following the financial crisis and the deficit reduction plan set out by the Westminster Government. Estimates provided to the Independent Budget Review (IBR) by the Scottish Government's Chief Economic Adviser – based on analysis of the Westminster Government's Budget in June 2010 – indicate that the resources controlled by the Scottish Government are projected to fall by 3.3 per cent per year on average in real terms over the next four years.[1] In total, the Scottish Government's departmental (DEL) budget is expected to reduce by £3.7 billion or 12.5 per cent over the next Spending Review period to 2014-15. This represents the largest reduction in spending since the Second World War. This reduction in spending is comparatively greater in Scotland than it is in the rest of the UK, since the Scottish Government's budget has increased by 5-6 per cent a year over the past decade.

11. Given the size of the total UK deficit, this reduction is likely to be sustained for many years. According to the Chief Economic Adviser, real terms budgets may not climb back to their 2009-10 level until 2025-26 (if indeed they ever do).[2] This equates to £42 billion less in total spending between 2010-11 and 2025-26 – equivalent to nearly four years' spending on NHS Scotland.[3]

12. Despite the size of these likely reductions in spending – and the difficulty there will be in achieving them – it should also be noted that they would broadly return Scotland to the levels

of spending on public services that existed just over ten years ago. On these projections, the Scottish Government will have a total departmental (DEL) budget of £28.1 billion (£25.6 billion in real terms) in 2014-15.[4] The fundamental question is not only how reductions in spending will be achieved, it is also how the resources available to Scotland are spent most effectively.

13. The analysis in this section suggests that the radical reform of Scotland's public services will need to form a part of the Scottish Government's approach to reducing public spending: firstly, because of the policy options available to the Scottish Government; secondly, because even with significant additional investment, Scottish public services have been struggling to meet rising demands.

The limits of efficiencies and reductions in provision
14. Any government has five basic options to reduce deficits (or in the case of Scotland, the gap between current levels of spending and its anticipated allocation from the Westminster Government):

- Relying on future economic growth to increase revenues from taxation.
- Raising additional taxation revenue.
- Achieving efficiencies within existing programmes and services (without reinvesting these savings in other areas).
- Reducing and/or halting some existing programmes and services.
- The radical reform of programmes and services to reduce costs.

In most cases, governments will rely on some combination of these five. The potential of these options for Scotland is discussed below.

15. The Independent Budget Review (IBR) has determined that there are no current forecasts for economic growth that would allow Scotland to grow its way out of the problem within the timeframe of Spending Review 2010 (2011-12 to 2014-15).[5] The situation could be even more difficult if the UK enters a 'double-

dip' recession.

16. For political and economic reasons, raising significant additional revenue is not a realistic option for Scotland. The IBR notes the UK Government's calculation that a one penny change in the Scottish variable rate (SVR) could be worth approximately plus or minus £350 million in 2010-11 and plus or minus £400 million in 2011-12. The IBR also notes the potential for charging for some currently free provision; this is examined below.

17. Scotland has made progress in achieving its efficiency savings target of 2 per cent per annum over the three-year period 2008 to 2011, amounting to £1.6 billion in total (the latest Efficiency Delivery Plan suggests that future savings could again be in excess of the target, as was achieved in 2008-09).[6] Yet even with savings in excess of the target, efficiencies are only likely to play a partial role in bridging the funding gap. As the IBR notes, achieving the current 2 per cent efficiency target year-on-year could generate savings (excluding pay and capital) in the last year of the next Spending Review period (2014-15) of approximately £600 million (3 per cent would generate savings of £900 million).

18. In addition, the Simplification Programme will provide an estimated net financial saving of £123 million during 2008-13 and annual recurring savings of £36 million thereafter.[7] Further, the Public Procurement Reform Programme has generated (cash and non-cash) savings of £327 million over the same period. Lastly, in 2008-09, £160 million of cash-releasing savings were realised through procurement.

19. The remaining funding gap will force the Scottish Government and Scotland's public services to reduce and/or halt some existing programmes and services. Currently, much of the debate in Scotland has focused on which programmes and services, including the implications of 'protecting' some areas of spending.[8] A particular issue with the IBR (and of the current debate more generally) is that it has adopted a primarily 'static' view of these choices, for example, which entitlements might be abolished or frozen.

20. While this is a necessary and important part of the

debate, it has two main limitations. First, such reductions may be necessary but they will not be sufficient. The IBR notes a range of money-saving options and calculates the savings they could achieve. For example, raising the age of entitlement for concessionary travel from 60 to 65 (and subsequently in line with retirement age) would produce £279 million in estimated savings by 2014-15. Reducing free personal care payments to £100 per week produces £120 million by the same year. Introducing prescription charges or charging for some NHS eye examinations would generate around £128 million and £93 million respectively.[9]

21. These are highly contentious options, likely to have negative consequences for other public services. The IBR has prompted considerable debate between Scottish political parties on the viability and legitimacy of these options. The Scottish Government has already rejected some of the options discussed, including proposals to alter the eligibility criteria for concessionary travel and personal care payments and ending the freeze on Council Tax payments.

22. Yet even if all of the measures costed in the IBR were publicly acceptable and enacted quickly, they only achieve around three-quarters of the required reductions in spending. This would still leave Scotland needing to find a further £1 billion in spending reductions by 2014-15.[10] Such figures should prompt to focus the debate in Scotland away from the viability of specific entitlements (important though this is) and towards the much larger issue of the overall sustainability of Scotland's public services.

23. Second, any reductions (whether of the types discussed above or general reductions in service provision) need to be judged not only in terms of how much they might save in the short-term, but also their likely social impact, whether they protect the most vulnerable and how this might affect other public services – for example, how the abolition of an entitlement might have the effect of merely displacing costs from one service to another.

24. Reductions in spending could also have a significant impact on the economy. Government spending in Scotland represents a proportionately larger part of the economy than it does for

the UK as a whole,[11] as does employment in the public sector,[12] and so reductions could have a greater impact on economic recovery following the recession.[13] The recession has in some respects had a deeper impact on Scotland than in other parts of the UK, raising levels of unemployment and area-based inequalities. The result of ill-judged reductions in spending on the economy and society could be a deep 'social recession', whereby the economic recession is followed by a vicious circle of rising demand for public services but fewer resources.

25. Given the limits of the first four options, the debate in Scotland also needs to include the radical reform of public services and how this might play an important role in both saving money and maintaining (and even improving) the outcomes from Scotland's public services. As the IBR itself noted, the scale of the reductions required means that the debate will also have to include the transformation of the organisation and delivery of public services in Scotland to meet future needs. Indeed, the more that radical reform plays a role in reducing spending and improving outcomes, the less emphasis might need to be placed on other contentious and potentially harmful measures.

26. Radical reform does not mean avoiding difficult decisions. If new approaches are to save money, they must enable reduced spending in some aspects of existing provision (and by more than it costs to develop and implement reform). Savings can derive from shifting resources to other approaches, reducing demand by introducing effective new approaches, changing levels of entitlements, over time reducing the number of public service employees within existing organisations, reducing the scope of (or in some cases abolishing) some existing organisations, and lower procurement spending on goods and supplies. The sources of potential savings from radical reform are further identified in Part 2.

The social challenge

27. If radical reform is to play an important part in reducing spending, logically it needs to focus on the major drivers of costs for public services. Despite the important reforms of the past ten years – and the commitment of thousands of public

service professionals and carers – Scotland faces a series of long-term challenges as a result of changing demands for public services. These changing demands are set to continue, further pushing up costs. But this also helps to identify where, with more effective interventions, there is the potential for major savings.

28. In some areas, significant investment in public services has produced improved results. For example, there has been slightly better progress in reducing child poverty rates in Scotland over the past ten years than in the rest of the UK.[14] Yet as is reflected in other parts of the UK and OECD countries, the changing nature of demand is putting pressure on current models for delivering public services.

29. High rates of poverty, income inequality and social exclusion in Scotland have a corresponding effect on demand for services and many social issues are intimately linked to socioeconomic circumstance.[15] In 2008-09, 17 per cent of Scots (860,000 people) were living in relative poverty (before housing costs).[16] There are indicators that circumstances may now be even more challenging for many in Scotland following the recession, giving rise to further demand for services.[17] Rising and increasingly complex demand is a particular challenge in areas of health, social care and justice – three areas which are the focus of this paper.

30. Scotland has made significant investment in health care provision and spends proportionally more than rest of the UK; £1,963 per capita compared to £1,772.[18] The bold introduction of the smoking ban in 2006 has led to a reduction in heart and lung condition rates and improved public health.[19] Yet, despite some improvements, overall Scotland's health remains poor in comparison to its OECD counterparts. Life expectancy remains low compared to many European countries. The following table compares the health and wellbeing of Scotland to the UK as a whole and also to Finland (as a similarly sized nation of 5.4 million people).

Table 1: Selected health indicators for Scotland, the UK and Finland, most recent comparative data[20]

Health indicator	Scotland	UK	Finland
Ischaemic heart disease-related deaths per 100,000 people (ages 0-64) (2007)[21]	32.64	22.98	25.33
Respiratory disease-related deaths per 100,000 people (2007)	85.71	73.39	25.84
Diabetes-related deaths per 100,000 people (2007)	9.33	6.43	6.75
Alcohol-related deaths per 100,000 people (2007)	75.45	51.02	93.73
Smoking-related deaths per 100,000 people (2007)	285.98	223.17	229.52
Life expectancy at birth, years (2006)	77.36	79.66	79.68

Source: Scotland and European Health for All (HfA) Database 2009.

31. It is increasingly long-term conditions and their consequences that are the dominant (cost) pressure for NHS Scotland. People living with long-term conditions such as coronary heart disease, cardiovascular disease, Type 2 diabetes and low-level mental health conditions account for 80 per cent of all GP consultations.[22] People with these conditions are twice as likely to be admitted to hospital, will stay in hospital disproportionately longer and account for over 60 per cent of hospital bed days used.[23]

32. These conditions tend to be affected by socioeconomic conditions, behaviours such as excessive drinking, unhealthy diet and lack of exercise, and are closely related to issues of poverty and inequality. More than two-thirds of the total alcohol-related deaths were in the most deprived two-fifths

of areas and the so-called 'Scottish Effect' of higher-than-expected mortality has been attributed in part to rates of drug abuse across Scotland.[24] UK-wide data adjusted for Scotland suggest that long-term conditions cost NHS Scotland £1.74 billion each year in 2007, and that this will increase to £2.15 billion by 2025 (an increase of £410 million a year).[25] This amounts to around £4 billion in additional costs for NHS Scotland between now and 2025.

33. The Scottish Government has made a progressive commitment to ensuring adequate social care is provided for those in need. Yet as in other parts of the UK, projected demands derived from an ageing population will outpace realistically available resources.[26] In 2008, 16.4 per cent of the Scottish population were 65 and over, compared with 16 per cent for the UK as a whole.[27] This section of the population is projected to increase by 21 per cent between 2006 and 2016, and will be 62 per cent bigger by 2031.[28] For those aged 85 and over, the population will rise by 38 per cent by 2016 and 144 per cent by 2031. This is particularly significant, as the need for care is far greater amongst over-85 year olds.

34. Scotland currently spends £4.5 billion a year on providing health and care services for those over 65 years; £1.4 billion (30 per cent) of this goes on emergency hospital admissions. By 2016, the number of older Scots requiring some form of care is expected to rise by up to a quarter, rising to nearly two-thirds by 2032.[29] If Scotland continues to provide services in the same way, current spending will need to increase by £1.1 billion by 2016, and by £3.5 billion, or 74 per cent, by 2031.[30]

35. Criminal justice is another area where rising demand for services is unsustainable given limits to supply. Though crime rates in Scotland have broadly decreased over the past decade, Scotland's prison population has increased by 31 per cent.[31] Despite the fact that over 85 per cent of convictions result in non-custodial sentences, there are currently around 7,900 people in Scottish prisons – more than they were intended to accommodate. In 2008, over 75 per cent of all custodial convictions were for six months or less (and half were only for a three-month period). The two-year reconviction rate has remained the same over the last few years, at 45 per cent for

the 2005-06 cohort.[32]

36. The Scottish Prison Service is expected to cost £485.9 million in 2010-11 (of which £349 million is current and £136.9 million is capital expenditure).[33] On current rates of growth, the prison population would be expected to rise to 9,600 prisoners by 2018-19.[34] The Scottish Consortium on Crime and Criminal Justice has conducted an analysis based on a long-range projection of 10,500 prisoners by 2030 (11,900 if the changes proposed in the Custodial Sentencing and Weapons (Scotland) Act are implemented)[35] and estimated that these numbers could require seven new prisons and see the cost of prisons rise by £200-£250 million a year to nearly £700 million a year (a total additional cost of more than £6 billion over the following 25 years).[36]

37. As with health, there is a strong relationship between crime and anti-social behaviour and poverty and inequality. Research into the concentration of prisoners in Scottish prisons found that a considerable number of inmates came from the same few communities. In 2003, a quarter of prisoners in Scotland's jails came from just 50 of 1,222 council wards. Furthermore, 1 in 29 of all 23 year old men from these communities was in prison.[37]

38. The data presented here suggest that Scotland faces additional demands in these three areas of public service provision alone amounting to more than £27 billion in the next 15 years – the period in which there is likely to be £42 billion less to spend. This suggests that Scotland's public services are currently unsustainable without radical reform to ensure that they are both more effective and efficient. 'Sustainable' public services are those that are both affordable and garner widespread support from the public. Reductions in spending are likely to reduce provision for services that are struggling to meet current demand, let alone projected future demand. Understandably, public satisfaction with services could decline markedly.[38]

PART 2:
HOW RADICAL REFORM IN PUBLIC SERVICES CAN REDUCE DEMAND AND IMPROVE OUTCOMES

39. Over the past ten years, Scotland has introduced some significant reforms to public services that have differed from developments in the rest of the UK (and England in particular). Successive Scottish Governments have done much to increase provision of free universal services, including free personal and nursing care at home for the elderly, free prescriptions, eye tests, dental checks and concessionary travel.

40. The principles of universal services has stemmed from a critique of selectivity on the grounds that means-tested or needs-based provision brings stigma to those who may be deemed eligible and increases the possibility of multiple levels of service.[39] Free pre-school places for all three and four year olds is a central tenet of Scottish Early Years policy, while Scotland no longer has tuition fees in higher education. Across all public services in Scotland, the Local Government Concordat and Single Outcome Agreements have encouraged a sharper focus on what services ought to achieve as a driver for improvement.[40]

41. Despite this, public services in Scotland (as elsewhere) still tend to be organised and monitored in terms of 'inputs' – levels of spending, the size of the public sector workforce and organisational structures. The focus of reform has been largely on the 'supply-side', in the sense of what services are delivered and by whom.

42. The forthcoming limits to 'supply' following the Westminster Government's Comprehensive Spending Review mean that it is now critical to re-focus reform towards saving money (reducing inputs). But this does not mean neglecting outcomes; quite the opposite. In order to produce sustainable savings in public services, reform needs to focus on the major drivers of cost. This is to say, in order to save money the focus of reform needs to shift from what is supplied (and who supplies it) to how to manage and reduce demand through innovation. Delivering services in ways which best ensure the outcomes needed by service users should be at the core of reform.

The changing nature of the demand for services requires a different focus to reform

43. Some of the most urgent (and expensive) pressures on public services are demands that have traditionally been hard to meet through largely uniform provision. Across the UK, despite decades of reform, capital investment, and relentless effort on the part of professionals, the way that public services are organised today is still largely a legacy of the post-war welfare settlement and the more market-oriented changes of the 1980s – of relatively standardised services delivered to a mainly passive public.[41]

44. However, people's needs have changed. Conditions such as those associated with obesity, entrenched inequalities, and high rates of re-offending are complex, behavioural conditions that are strongly affected by lifestyle factors and social and economic circumstances. They cannot be easily 'fixed' by standardised packages of provision. The rising costs of these demands, as analysed in Part 1, indicate the relative failure of existing service models to respond to them.

45. Mainstream service delivery remains largely designed to react to problems rather than to prevent and solve them. Current and projected rising demand is then a function of increasingly ineffective models of service delivery (or models that are struggling to meet new and changing needs). The data presented in Part 1 suggest that the issue isn't only the amount of money that is spent on services (an input). It is also how

effective services are at helping people to meet their needs (that is, the outcome).

46. The dominant tendency in public services has been towards incremental reform and improvement, rather than a more fundamental reorganisation of a new 'welfare settlement' that better meets people's needs at cheaper cost. If Scotland is to reduce spending without harming its economy and society, radical reform in public services needs to become a more significant part of the strategy towards spending reductions. In particular, new approaches need to be developed and implemented that are much more effective in managing and reducing demand.

47. The key to making this shift is to recognise that the way services are designed and delivered is crucial to how they can reduce demand. In order to do this, services need to meet people's needs more effectively, and/or help them rely on services less by building their own capabilities to prevent and respond to problems themselves. There are some areas of provision where these sorts of approaches will obviously not be appropriate, such as transport services and infrastructure. However, there is considerable scope for more of these sorts of approaches in areas of service delivery where a significant proportion of demand stems from complex, behavioural conditions that rely on public engagement.

48. This focus serves as a basic definition of 'radical innovation' – the development and implementation of distinctively new approaches in public services that seek to manage and reduce demand more effectively (and so prove cheaper) than existing approaches. Radical innovation is especially appropriate in health, justice and social care, addressed in turn below.

Re-balancing health towards more preventative interventions

49. In health, the predominant model of care needs to shift from acute, hospital-based care to more preventative interventions.[42] This is especially important given the major demographic trends that are the predominant drivers of health expenditure.[43] Effective prevention policies have been shown

to reduce health inequalities and address the disproportionate costs of high intensity users within the health service.[44] Developing self-management skills amongst people with long-term conditions has shown to be effective in alleviating these costs and reducing the rate of unelected admissions that can result.[45]

50. The Scottish Government has started to develop a more preventative, community-based strategy to tackle Scotland's health issues. The recent *Better Health, Better Care* White Paper set out a route-map towards a 'mutual NHS' in Scotland, involving the public not just as consumers of health services but as 'owners', with rights and responsibilities in improving health.[46] Scotland has made a concerted effort to integrate mental health improvement into health policy and has based its approach on a social model and understanding of mental health as highly influenced by our social networks and circumstance.[47] The introduction of Community Health Partnerships and the emphasis on community-based care followed the recommendations of the Kerr Report for more targeted service provision – and better integration between health and social care providers – to tackle the persistent health and socio-economic inequalities across Scotland.[48]

51. Nonetheless, the large majority of health spending still goes on acute care rather than preventative measures. In 2008-9, less than 4 per cent of health expenditure across the UK was spent on prevention.[49] Adult mental health costs government across the UK £10 billion each year in benefit payments alone, yet only £2 million is spent on prevention and alleviation, such as promoting self-esteem and coping skills.[50]

52. There are large-scale examples of where the necessary shift has been achieved. During the 1970s, Finland faced extremely high rates of coronary heart disease (CHD) and amongst the lowest life expectancy in the OECD. Prompted by a petition from the local people, the Finnish Government launched a major community-based initiative to prevent the development of these conditions by targeting the lifestyles of the whole population in a local area, not just those at high-risk. The 'North Karelia Project' drew on the expertise of grassroots and community organisations to understand the barriers to healthy

living and devolved responsibility for acting on them to the communities themselves. This meant that solutions were more appropriate to tackle the complex aspects of public health improvement and more effective at prevention.

53. The project targeted four key risk factors in order to reduce cardiovascular mortality: dietary changes, lowering smoking rates, reducing high blood pressure, and increasing physical activity. The approach achieved a significant reduction in health expenditure; by 2002, the annual CHD mortality rate amongst men had reduced by 75 per cent, lung cancer rates were 70 per cent lower, and life expectancy had increased by six years for men and seven years for women.[51]

54. It is important to recognise that health improvement in Finland during this period would have been influenced by other factors such as the growth of the economy and employment generally and advances in health care and technology. However, evidence suggests that the targeted, multi-agency intervention in North Karelia was able to affect public behaviour in a sustainable and supportive way and that the health of the area was more markedly improved than other parts of Finland.[52] The project has since expanded across Finland and has been used as a basis for a number of health prevention initiatives internationally.[53] Evidence of success indicates that a well-planned, inclusive, community-based prevention programme can have an enormous impact on lifestyle to improve health and life chances within communities.[54]

55. The community-based, integrated approach of the North Karelia Project is reflected in the Healthy Weight Community Projects, being developed in a number of local authorities across Scotland. Rapidly rising rates of obesity – particularly amongst children – are an increasing concern, with direct costs to NHS Scotland estimated to be in excess of £175 million (with costs projected to almost double by 2030).[55] Based explicitly on France's 'EPODE' (Ensemble, Prévenons l'Obésité des Enfants) Programme to tackle childhood obesity – which managed to reduce obesity rates by 25 per cent in participating areas – the project aims to harness community efforts to make healthier food choices and encourage more physical activity in everyday life. North Lanarkshire Council is one area taking

part, where the Council is focusing efforts in linking families, nurseries and schools to promote healthy eating and exercise.[56]

56. Similarly, the intensive, inter-agency approach is an important feature of West Dunbartonshire's integrated scheme to reduce smoking in the local area. Forty per cent of residents smoke in the Whitecrook neighbourhood near Clydebank, leading the Council to bid to become one of Scotland's 'Equally Well' Test Sites, a structured programme to reduce inequality in local health and wellbeing. Different smoking cessation initiatives pitched at different audiences simultaneously will test a collaborative, joined-up approach to prevention targeted at a local area. Other places are testing new approaches to reducing health inequalities through improving wellbeing, access to employment and skills development and community regeneration. With encouragement to learn across areas, the Equally Well sites aim to cultivate the conditions for service redesign and integration, agreeing shared outcomes across a number of agencies and developing services that look and feel different for service users.[57]

57. There are many examples of voluntary or community-based health initiatives to improve health across Scotland, ranging from the British Trust for Conservation Volunteers 'Green Gyms' that combine gardening and conservation work with physical activity and community action, to larger-scale programmes such as the Dundee Healthy Living Initiative, a community-led initiative to promote wellbeing and reduce health inequalities. The ongoing Pilton Community Health Project, a charity that runs a number of community health projects with NHS Lothian and the City of Edinburgh Council, promotes community engagement in targeting mental health, improved diet and physical activity. Some of the more remote parts of Scotland have a particular incentive to make use of community assets and networks in promoting health given the challenges of remote provision.[58]

58. Nonetheless, these sorts of public health initiatives tend to be marginalised as health promotion activities, and could be identified as 'soft targets' for spending reductions. Important though health promotion is, it is short of a broader and more radical re-interpretation of public health that would rebalance

care away from acute care towards more community-based and led initiatives to health and wellbeing. As the nature of demand for health services changes following the trends set out in Part 1, there is scope for more rigorous, structured approaches to community-led prevention and health care.

59. Effective preventative measures can also be applied to drug and alcohol abuse. An estimated 52,000 people in Scotland are problem drug-users, and drug and alcohol-related deaths are amongst the highest in Europe.[59] As noted in Part 1, poor health and health inequalities are tied to social and economic circumstance and can be affected by these sorts of behavioural or habitual factors. Audit Scotland has estimated that the wider costs to society of drug and alcohol abuse amount to almost £5 billion (of which £3.4 billion is borne directly by public services).[60]

60. There are a number of local authorities in Scotland that have made progress in developing integrated approaches to drug and alcohol intervention that prevent or better manage addiction, in line with the Scottish Government's commitment to better prevention through a 'recovery approach'.[61]

61. In Dumfries and Galloway for example, the Sunrise Project was commissioned by the local Alcohol and Drug Action Team (ADAT) to encourage uptake of services and early intervention through coordinated support from a number of agencies including NHS Scotland, Drug and Alcohol Support services and the voluntary organisation Turning Point. By rebalancing the provision of support from statutory to non-statutory services, Sunrise has enabled a reduction in demand for medical help. With more people entering and staying in rehabilitation and progressively more services being provided by voluntary services, the newly adopted Integrated Drugs Service – designed following evaluation of the Sunrise project – has dramatically increased its capacity for supporting the more extreme cases (from capacity for 70 clients to near 200).[62]

62. In Aberdeen, the drug treatment charity 'Phoenix Futures' has been working with the local authority and a number of other partners to provide coordinated, specialist support for drug users at a community level. The Integrated Drug Service Community Rehabilitation (IDSCR) programme offers people

a package of co-ordinated support and specialist interventions around drugs, housing, employment and training. The programme provides service users with a key contact across a range of services and users have the opportunity to participate in a range of community activities – volunteering, attending social and training sessions and rehabilitation.[63]

63. Yet there remains scope for more radical approaches – such as those that involve users directly in service design and delivery – to achieve more complete transformation of drugs services. Working with drug service providers in West Sussex in England, the RSA trained service users in research and evaluation techniques to understand the needs of other users in the community, and designed services to meet them. The proposals for new services emphasised the value of peer and community support, 'recovery communities' to strengthen collective resilience and strength against addiction as well as better signposting and personalisation. Placing users at the centre of the design process also increases the likelihood of effective intervention and compliance.[64]

64. In 2007-08, Scotland spent £173 million directly on managing the effects of drug and alcohol abuse.[65] The large majority of this is spent on treatment and care services, with only 6 per cent applied to prevention. For illustrative purposes, if a proportion of this spending were redirected towards more effective prevention measures that reduce the wider costs of drug and alcohol abuse by only 1 per cent, this could suggest savings of around £50 million each year for Scotland.

Redesigning social care to draw on and build community resources

65. Social care is another area subject to changing demands and expectations. As demographics shift, it will become increasingly important to ensure that care is provided in the most appropriate, personal way that can effectively respond to local needs. Support for the 'young old' will vary from support for the most aged; support will also be shaped by the urban or rural context. Meaningful engagement of service users to help meet diverse needs will be an important aspect of the future of care.[66]

66. The Reshaping Care for Older People programme has made significant progress in re-thinking provision. Led by the Scottish Government, NHS Scotland and COSLA, the programme is an example of a strategic and innovative approach to re-designing services for older people, strengthened by an emphasis on stakeholder and public engagement. Work so far indicates a likely shift in the balance of care away from hospital settings, providing the necessary support and treatment in or close to home, helping people remain safe, confident and able to look after themselves. This shift includes more 'anticipatory' and preventative approaches, increased support for volunteer and community carers as well as a greater scope for self-care, often supported by technology.

67. The shift in the shape of social care – from an emphasis on standardised services towards supporting independence – is an example of a broader approach to public service reform that has come to be known as 'co-production'. Co-production demonstrates how services could achieve more if they were able to draw on people's existing networks and resources and build skills for self-management. Co-production approaches are based on the principles of shared decision-making and designing services with users and the public. Increasing evidence suggests that co-production can improve people's experience of public services and can improve their independence, thereby reducing costs.[67]

68. At the moment however, social care remains focused on institutional care. Over 60 per cent of Scottish Government spending on care for older people is on care in hospitals and care homes, and almost one-third is spent on emergency or unelected admissions (around £1.4 billion a year). Only 6.7 per cent of the budget is allocated to providing care at home.[68]

69. Instead, social care services should build people's capabilities and wellness in older age, rather than reacting when need becomes most acute.[69] This was the step taken through the introduction of Local Area Coordinators (LACs) in Western Australia in order to re-balance the provision of care from expensive, residential services to cheaper, community-based services that are better for the user.

70. LACs act as a local point of contact in communities and

organise a range of care services around a service user. The LAC tries to match the personal needs of service users within a particular area to what local providers, existing social networks and community assets can offer. The approach is designed to help people remain independent build specialist skills for self-management and to strengthen relationships.

71. With the introduction of LACs, Western Australia realised a 35 per cent cost saving from traditional social service-led approaches. Per capita costs were only A$3,316 per LAC given their broad geographical spread and the low set-up costs of the programme. From their position within the community, LACs were able to access traditionally hard-to-reach people and encourage take-up of preventative services.[70]

72. Some areas in Scotland have already adopted LACs as part of their strategy to improve independent living and draw on other community providers to offer their support services. North Lanarkshire Council has introduced LACs alongside a broader package of self-directed support to help people stay out of statutory care services by connecting them to local networks and support. By decentralising the coordination of services, developing a deeper and more personal relationship with service users and simplifying access to care, LACs are having a radical effect on the way services are organised, and the lives of the people who use them.

73. The coordinator role so critical to the LAC approach shares characteristics with the 'key worker' function in Partners for Inclusion, a successful approach to delivering support to individuals with mental or physical disabilities in Scotland. Partners for Inclusion assists service users throughout Ayrshire, Renfrewshire and East Renfrewshire to access the full range of available services, including community services, local social networks and the relationships within people's lives.

74. Partners for Inclusion works with users with complex needs who have found it difficult to navigate existing service provision and co-design a personalised care package with them. The charity then recruits someone (sometimes even a family member) to provide the relevant care. Partners for Inclusion also develops links with local businesses to scope employment opportunities and raise awareness of disability and

mental health accessibility. The annual cost of providing this integrated, personalised care has been estimated at £70,000, over 50 per cent less than the cost of a traditional residential care package.[71]

75. Further, West Lothian Council has started to demonstrate how telecare and telehealth technologies can help people remain independent and stay out of institutional care. Recently, West Lothian's Community Health and Care Partnership (CHCP) has developed an electronic self assessment tool – 'Safe at Home' – that has expert knowledge built in to calculate and provide a prescription of services targeted to the specific service user. The Council has integrated telecare services and a 'home health' approach into delivery across health and care services. Telecare solutions have reduced pressure on the health authority and West Lothian has estimated the cost of the care package to be over 60 per cent lower than the cost of providing care in an institutional setting.[72]

76. In Renfrewshire, the Council for Community Services and a number of community volunteers have developed a social approach to delivering forms of support for older people. Reaching Older People in Renfrewshire (ROAR) is a local mentoring and befriending service for older people, actively connecting them into a community and skills exchange. The service helps to address issues of social isolation that can affect people with dementia and early stages of Alzheimer's.

77. The service shares some of the social aspects characteristic of co-production. Timebanks, for example, are a vehicle for skills exchange and social interaction. Timebanks are reciprocal volunteering schemes, occasionally attached to local public services. In the Highlands, timebanks in Inverness, Lochaber and Badenoch and Stathspey are offering a way for people to get involved in community activities. Timebanks are an effective way of creating incentives for participation and activity which can have both physical and emotional benefits. Where timebanks have been attached to GP Practices for example, they can incentivise healthy lifestyles and behaviour. Rushey Green GP Practice in South London was able to achieve a 50 per cent reduction in the cost of GP consultations by redirecting demand for resources towards the timebank.[73]

78. As noted in Part 1, Scotland currently spends £4.5 billion a year on providing care for older people, £1.4 billion of which is spent on unplanned or emergency admissions. Even a 10 per cent reduction in the cost of unelected admissions – achieved through anticipatory or preventative care or supporting self-management as demonstrated in these examples – could achieve £140 million of savings each year.

Re-orientating criminal justice from 'containment' to reducing offending

79. The criminal justice system is struggling to cope with levels of offending; instead, it could be radically re-orientated towards reducing offending behaviour.[74] Motivations for offending often stem from a complex mix of personal experience and circumstance, mental health conditions, drug and alcohol abuse and peer influence, but early intervention and 'restorative' approaches have shown significant potential in preventing and reducing rates of offending.[75]

80. Limits to institutional capacity in Scotland make the need for a new approach urgent. The Scottish Prisons Commission in 2008 recommended an eventual reduction of the prison population to 5,000 prisoners and greater investment in community options in order to reduce crime.[76] In August 2010, a Parliamentary statutory instrument introduced a presumption against prison sentences of three months or less, with a view to reducing the pressures on the Scottish Prison Service by changing the 'supply' – by limiting the large numbers of prisoners who may only be in custody for very short periods and for whom the prospect of a prison sentence has little deterrent effect. It also aims to stop the cycle of re-offending which short-term sentences can perpetuate.[77]

81. Yet there remains further scope for interventions on the 'demand-side'. The growth of the prison population – and the geographical patterns of offending behaviour concentrated in different parts of Scotland – point to multidimensional aspects of offender management and the local conditions that can lead to disruptive behaviour. Housing services, education, children's services all have an important role in tackling crime, alongside

community justice providers, the voluntary sector, the police and victim support.[78]

82. Evidence from the US suggests that a bold strategic approach to diverting spending from containing to preventing problems can save money and improve outcomes. Faced with a rapidly expanding prison population, state officials in Texas rejected plans to spend $500 million on constructing a new prison and instead invested the money in tackling root causes of crime. The approach became known as Justice Reinvestment, redirecting spending from capital or institutional investment towards rehabilitation and earlier intervention at a community level.

83. Texas redirected half of the money set aside for the new prison on expanding residential and out-patient treatment centres for mental health, substance abuse and post-prison support. Parole revocations saw a 25 per cent drop and the prison population increased by 90 per cent less than anticipated. Texas estimated savings of $201.5 million in 2008-09, with savings from averted prison construction of an additional $233 million.[79]

84. Justice Reinvestment enabled investment in rehabilitative, preventative interventions because it saved money through capital disinvestment. This approach is relevant to Scotland given the strain on institutional capacity and the early indications of the success of alternative approaches.[80] Reinvesting the resources diverted from capital spending into community approaches allowed the State of Texas to grow the capacity of local, community services and social enterprises in delivering services to prevent offending.

85. There are examples of these sorts of community-based intervention that have demonstrated successful impact in Scotland. East Renfrewshire Council's School, Social Work, Police and Community (SSPC) programme, for example, is an innovative approach to prevent and break out of cycles of crime and anti-social behaviour. The programme brings together all local agencies involved in tackling youth offending alongside the offenders and their families to address the inter-generational and social aspects of violent and anti-social behaviour. It designs appropriate activities suited to the young

person to offer a route out of negative social networks or influences.

86. East Renfrewshire Council was able to reduce levels of crime across the local authority area: the number of people carrying weapons, referrals and vandalism incidents all dropped by over 20 per cent within two years. There was also a reduction in the number of persistent offenders during the period – one of the lowest and most improved results in Scotland.[79]

87. Evaluations of these sorts of restorative justice practices by the Ministry of Justice have found an average fall of 27 per cent in re-offending rates. The Restorative Justice Consortium estimates that for every £1 spent on restorative 'Conferences' (where the offender, their family and peers are brought together to map out a plan to prevent re-offending – not unlike East Renfrewshire) saves £9 in reconviction costs.[82] Given the current re-offending rate, achieving this kind of improvement could make significant savings.[83]

88. Programmes that effectively target communities with a high prevalence of crime have also demonstrated a positive economic and social impact. With an estimated 170 gangs operating in the city – more than operating in London, a city six times the size – Glasgow has the highest overall crime rate out of all local authority areas in Scotland.[84] At over 34 serious assaults per 10,000 people, serious assault in Glasgow is more than two and half times the national rate. Stabbings in the city account for half of all murders in Scotland and more than 50 per cent of knives found in Scotland are seized in Glasgow.[85] Again, drug and alcohol abuse are significant factors. There are fewer than 117 beds in drug rehabilitation centres in Glasgow, despite there being 40,000 addicts residing in the city (given the lack of rehabilitation, there is an emphasis on prescribing methadone, and nearly half of all Scotland's methadone users live in Glasgow).[86]

89. The Community Initiative to Reduce Violence (CIRV) was a two-year intensive programme with the aim of dramatically reducing gang violence in Glasgow's East End. Practitioners engaged directly with gang members in groups, using peer influence as a way to encourage positive behaviour change.

A total of £5 million was invested in the project which over an 18-month evaluation period has seen an average 46 per cent reduction in the level of violent offending by the 368 gang members who engaged with the programme. The peer approach also enabled an 18.5 per cent reduction in violent offending by members who refused to engage.[87]

90. The Scottish Prison Service is budgeted to cost £485.9 million in 2010-11, including £136.8 million in capital costs.[88] If a small proportion of this spend was reinvested into approaches such as Glasgow's Community Initiative to Reduce Violence – that is, approaches that reduce demand for statutory services through better prevention – the impact across Scotland could be significant. A 10 per cent reduction in the costs of the prison system would suggest savings of approaching £50 million a year.

PART 3: TRANSFORMING SCOTLAND'S PUBLIC SERVICES

The need for innovation to meet the challenges facing Scotland's public services

91. If Scotland is to meet the need for savings without subsequent harm to its economy and society (or at least the extent to which it seems likely at present), radical innovation – led by a focus on saving money – needs to play a much more significant role in the strategy towards spending reductions. While we shouldn't underestimate the difficulties in reform, the scale and immediacy of the pressures faced by Scotland's public services should be used to provide the necessary impetus to radical thinking and bold action required at all levels in Scotland's public services, from national government to local providers.

92. As illustrated by the examples in Part 2, new approaches to delivering public services are already being put into practice in Scotland, in the rest of the UK and internationally. These approaches can save money and improve outcomes through better demand management, and thereby reducing costs for statutory services. The question is how the Scottish Government can stimulate and support the development and spread of new approaches that manage and reduce demand more effectively and ensure universally better outcomes for citizens.

93. This requires more innovation in Scotland – creating a greater appetite for new approaches and providing more support to develop and implement them, and help the successful ones spread. Even though some of these approaches

will be developed outside of existing public services (for example, by social enterprises), the state has a critical strategic role setting the direction of travel and in creating the right conditions for new approaches to be developed, through policy, regulation, performance measurement and audit, and funding and commissioning.

94. This will of course be particularly difficult in the context of the next few years of reductions in public spending. There will be an understandable tendency to either resist reductions or to try to save money from within existing services without affecting provision. However, as noted in Part 1, it is highly unlikely that efficiencies within existing services and/or reducing some services will achieve the scale of savings required, while also risking significant economic and social harm.

95. As public services represent a larger part of the economy in Scotland than they do in the UK as a whole, radical reform is even more important in Scotland to ensure that service models continue to meet changing demand. The alternative approach – incremental cuts to already struggling services – risks undermining the ability of services and staff to cope with current (let alone future) demands.

The conditions for radical innovation

96. As illustrated by the case studies included in Part 2, developing and delivering radical innovation requires the following conditions: a widespread culture and practice of local experimentation; incentives, investment and support; a strong 'social economy' of community organisations and social enterprises and a culture of partnership working in public services; and public engagement to inform, support and deliver change. These are discussed in turn below.

Local experimentation
97. Radical innovation requires a widespread culture and practice of local experimentation, with a greater capacity and relevant freedoms at a local level to develop and implement new approaches. Public services are of course primarily

delivered locally or by non-national organisations (such as local authorities and health boards). These are the organisations that need to implement reform, but it is now also vital that they develop and lead innovation.

98. This is for two main reasons. Firstly, there are limits to what constitutes supposedly generalisable 'best practice' in public services when social problems are intimately linked to how people live their lives and local circumstances. One of the most critical factors in the success of the East Renfrewshire approach, for example, was that it was locally managed and thus able to target interventions appropriately for the specific needs and circumstances of its community.[89]

99. Secondly, a greater variety of approaches can be valuable when specific social contexts, behaviours and personal networks have a demonstrable impact on people's actions and attitudes. Like the rest of the UK, Scotland already suffers from health and wealth inequalities between localities, due often to the particular features and circumstances of the area (urban development, access to employment and transport links, for example).[90]

100. For these reasons, more effective and efficient approaches in public services cannot be designed from the centre. The types of innovation that are now most important need to be developed by drawing on the expertise and insight of frontline workers and by working closely with users and communities.

101. The Local Government Concordat and Single Outcome Agreements have been an important step forward in providing local authorities with greater freedoms to allocate resources and design services that meet local needs and objectives. In addition, the Scottish Government has sought to reduce the burden of performance management regimes and audit generally.[91] This should continue as reductions in spending are made over the next few years.

102. While there are important 'pockets' of local innovation in Scotland at the moment, it is not sufficiently widespread or radical for the challenges facing public services now. In particular, local innovation requires a stronger sense of ownership by local providers, as well as more resourcing and

support.

103. The greater diversity of provision that is likely to result from more local experimentation naturally brings with it concerns regarding access and equity. These concerns might be greater in Scotland than in some other parts of the UK, given Scotland's traditional emphasis on universal and equitable provision and also because some of its population lives in very remote areas. Further, relatively high levels of poverty and income inequality in Scotland raise concerns that those living on low incomes or without easy access to services are appropriately provided for. However, these concerns should not inhibit the consideration of new approaches. Diversity doesn't necessarily undermine universality, and the broad goal of universally better outcomes shouldn't dictate uniform service provision, especially given the very different local conditions in some Scottish communities.

104. For example, Local Area Coordinators have been able to reduce spending on residential care services by drawing on the full range of local resources to meet the needs of the service user. The LAC's role becomes ensuring that public services get delivered, rather than necessarily delivering services themselves. Access to services has improved as a result; LACs have been able to access traditionally hard-to-reach service users and take-up of preventative services is 58 per cent higher than the national average.[92]

Incentives, investment and support

105. Local experimentation needs to be supported by a strong but more strategic role for central government. The role of central government (and politicians) should not be to 'micro-manage' local provision (for example, by intervening in agreed plans to change provision at a local level); rather it should be to create the best possible conditions for local providers to innovate.

106. This has two main aspects. Firstly, central government has a crucial role in setting out new strategic, long-term 'visions' for how public services need to act and look differently in the future. The larger-scale case studies highlighted in Part 2 (such as Justice Reinvestment) suggest that local innovation requires the centre (in this case, the state government of Texas) to

provide the leadership and indeed political 'cover' for radical change at a local level. Only central government can lead a national debate on the future of public services, especially the potentially controversial systemic shift from demand-led provision towards demand-managing and reducing approaches, and bring together the national organisations that represent public service providers in order to agree how in broad terms this shift will be achieved.

107. In this regard, Scotland has an advantage over some other parts of the UK in its comparatively cohesive and progressive political culture, smaller policymaking and senior decision-making community (through which, for example, there is the potential for new ideas and approaches to be shared and agreed more rapidly), relatively coherent outcomes frameworks on the basis of Single Outcome Agreements and a general desire to differentiate itself from approaches taken in some other countries.

108. There is of course a possible tension between strategic change led from the centre and the importance of locally led experimentation (and also between centrally led change and public engagement, discussed below). Nonetheless, these are issues that the Scottish Government and Scotland's public services will have to negotiate anyway over the next few years, whether in managing efficiencies, reductions in service provision or innovation. Engaging local public service providers and the public will be crucial either way. Because they also focus on improving outcomes, positive programmes of innovative reform stand a greater chance of engendering engagement and support than the alternatives.

109. Secondly, only central government can ensure that the necessary incentives, investment and support are available to local providers of public services in order for them to innovate. Given increasing budget allocations in many public services over the past few years (in Scotland but also across the UK), it is understandable that incentives and support have largely been focused on improvement and efficiency within existing models of service delivery, rather than the radical reform of these models. This will have to change if Scotland's public services are to be supported to focus much more on

innovation. The challenge now is to ensure that the appropriate incentives, investment and support are made available for radical innovation, during a period when resources will be much less available generally (we propose a specific mechanism for this below). Even so, it is worth noting that any private sector business that wants to create future market-leading products and services needs to invest in innovation – even in a recession when resources are constrained.

A strong social sector and a culture of partnership

110. Existing frameworks of Single Outcome Agreements and the Local Government Concordat already encourage partnership working and shared strategic priorities across local providers. Yet there remains scope for more effective partnership working across service areas, in particular between social care and health and between local authorities. Though mechanisms such as pooled budgets have been trialled in some areas – in Tayside between NHS Tayside and Perth and Kinross Council or in Clackmannanshire between community health services – these formal incentives need to be supported by a culture of partnership on the basis of shared objectives.[93]

111. Public services can also work more closely with the 'social sector' – social enterprises, charities and community organisations – which can be a powerful source of innovative responses to social problems and a source of new providers and resources.[94] Many of the innovations highlighted here depend on mainstream public service providers working in partnership with the social sector to develop new approaches and deliver them.

112. Such innovations draw on a wider variety of social resources than is typical for public services; this is an important reason why they are both better and cheaper than traditional approaches. Further, innovation in public services should aim to strengthen this social capital; stronger communities will be more able to develop solutions to their own problems, so reducing demand on public services and the state.

113. The Scottish Government has done much already to support the development of the third sector. Its Third Sector budget seeks to secure the progression of an innovative,

sustainable and inclusive third sector, to support more cohesive communities, contribute to public services and improve economic growth. The 2010-11 budget allocated £20.8 million for 'third sector development' and £14.8 million for the Scottish Investment Fund (a total of £35.6 million). The Scottish Investment Fund supports enterprise in the third sector by investing in assets, business development and the skills of people working in the sector. The budget also supports volunteering and a series of strategic partnerships with national third sector organisations aimed at building third sector capacity.

114. Given its potential to help improve public services and support communities, it is vital that programmes of support and investment for Scotland's social sector are not seen as 'soft targets' for reduced spending over the next few years. But it is also important that support for the social sector is not regarded as a separate activity to innovation in mainstream public services; for example, there is little point in investing in the development of the sector if it is unable to gain access to commissions for new services. Support for the social sector needs to be integrated with the stronger focus on locally led innovation; this might have implications for whether a centralised model of disbursing funding for the social sector is most appropriate.

Widespread public engagement
115. Given the need to make deep savings, there is a serious danger of concerted (and understandable) professional and public resistance to reductions in provision, even if it is part of a shift to alternative forms of provision. Yet many of these innovations highlighted here rely on ongoing public engagement, involvement and support – ranging from providing a mandate for reform to the public being involved themselves in developing and delivering new approaches (for example, through social sector organisations).

116. The public can be allies in transformation only if the need for change is discussed more openly and consistently, and if there are individual and collective opportunities for the public to be involved. This might also allow government and public service providers to be bolder in making more radical reforms.

117. There has been some consideration already about how greater public discussion (if not direct engagement per se) might be achieved at a national level. For example the IBR floated the idea of a Scottish Parliamentary cross-party working group supported by a specialist advisory team, or a working group of selected contributors, to consider the longer-term shape of public service provision in Scotland, reporting to the Government and Parliament after the election in 2011.

118. As part of the budgeting process in 2011-12, we propose a national, cross-party commission looking into how services should operate differently in the future. This commission would provide a strategic direction for radical reform, but it is also crucial that public engagement is developed at a local level to build the necessary understanding and ownership that better enables transformation.

The overall context: reduced budgets combined with radical reform

119. We propose an ambitious new way for local public services to lead the next stage of radical reform that saves money and improves outcomes for citizens. We propose new powers and responsibilities for leading authorities and public bodies that take forward the Concordat, Single Outcome Agreements and existing frameworks. This mechanism – explained in more detail below – would provide greater local agency for developing new approaches in public services that are both better and cheaper, guided and supported by national programmes of reform and reinvestment.

120. To set the context for locally led innovation, we propose that the Scottish Government sets out broad programmes (strategies) of radical reform in health, social care and justice, based on the Justice Reinvestment model of disinvestment and reinvestment discussed in Part 2. The point of the Justice Reinvestment model is that is does not require additional net investment; in this model, any funding for new approaches comes from progressively disinvesting in some existing provision and diverting a proportion of the savings to new cheaper, more effective approaches. This should be the case

with these programmes, within a commitment to reduce spending in each area overall.[95]

121. There should be three initial areas of focus for these reinvestment programmes: health, social care and justice. These should in effect act as 'platforms' that stimulate and support radical innovation by local providers. These programmes should begin in the next Spending Review period (2011-12 to 2014-15) but last beyond this in order to realise the fullest possible savings (probably through a ten-year delivery plan). Underpinning each of these programmes should be a fundamental shift in how services engage the public in order to manage (and reduce) demand more effectively. As noted in Part 2, there is already some agreement on the required direction of radical reform in these areas.

122. In health, the reinvestment programme should focus on a shift from management and acute care to more preventative interventions. A significant area for potential savings is from drug or alcohol abuse. While not underestimating the difficulties of reform and implementation, even a reduction of 1 per cent in the costs associated with drug and alcohol-related abuse would generate savings of around £200 million over the course of the next Spending Review period.

123. In social care, the reinvestment programme should build on the outcome from the Reshaping Care for Older People programme (for which the public engagement phase has just ended). There is significant scope in social care services to rebalance care away from predominantly institutional provision towards community-based care. For illustrative purposes, even a 10 per cent reduction in the cost of emergency hospital admissions each year would save £560 million during the next Spending Review period.

124. In justice, the reinvestment programme should be modelled directly on Justice Reinvestment, that is a shift from containment to prevention and rehabilitation. In this area, a 10 per cent reduction in the costs of the prison system would suggest savings of £200 million during the next Spending Review period.

125. These areas are at once the most important and

challenging areas for reform as health, justice and care services are amongst those the public cares about most. Radical reform or spending cuts in these areas is likely to be a highly visible and contested decision. However, the danger of insulating any area from reform is that these services are the least reformed, and so the most vulnerable to being overwhelmed by increasing demand. Services that play such a vital role in ensuring a productive and healthy society also need to develop better approaches to meeting changing needs.

126. These programmes would benefit from establishing a challenging headline (input or output) 'target' alongside wider outcome measures in order to drive change. The current target for the Reshaping Care programme is doubling the proportion of spending on care at home (currently 6.7 per cent). An equivalent headline target in justice might be the number of prison places removed from the system, for example. Such targets would help to 'raise the bar' for public services, stimulating responses that go beyond an improvement mindset and towards generating more radical innovation.

127. These programmes would of course have to be developed and agreed with the services themselves, such as NHS Scotland, COSLA (representing local authorities) and national justice authorities. Further, all of these programmes (albeit at a broad level) would also need to be subject to an equality impact assessment or equivalent evaluation to determine as far as possible how they will affect society.[96] Finally, these programmes would require public engagement for their development; again, the Reshaping Care for Older People programme provides a model here.

128. In the context of these programmes, the introduction of new local agreements as described below does not require additional net resources. Any investment is funded through these programmes of disinvestment in existing demand-led approaches and services.

A new offer to local public service providers: 'new community' status

129. We recommend the introduction of a 'new community' status that leading local public service providers could opt to apply for. New community status offers greater local agency investment and support for innovation, in return for a commitment to return a proportion of the projected savings from innovation to central government.[97] This status could be open to local providers for the next Spending Review period (2011-12 to 2014-15). Those providers who do not opt for this status would continue to operate under their current arrangements.[98]

130. We suggest that this status is initially open only to providers of services in health, social care or justice (that is, principally health boards, local authorities, and local justice agencies). This is for a number of reasons. With the addition of education, these sectors make up a significant proportion of spending on public services in Scotland. These sectors are obviously critical to the health, safety and productivity of Scotland's economy and society. Further, as noted in Part 2, there is the potential to save significant amounts of money by shifting provision in these areas towards approaches that manage and reduce demand more effectively – hence our proposal that the Scottish Government sets out broad programmes of radical reform in these areas.

131. We have considered whether such a status should be introduced across Scotland in one go, that is, whether it should become the norm for all public service providers. The argument against this is that some providers are better placed than others to embark on these types of innovation, because of their current performance, capability and expertise in reform, the strength of their local leadership, the extent of their existing community engagement and other local factors. For these reasons, it is more sensible at this stage for each provider to judge whether it is right for them. Other providers could of course choose to adopt the new approaches that are developed by new community providers as they wish. Further, if successful, new community status could become the normal relationship between local providers and central government

during the following Spending Review period (that is, post 2014-15).

Funding and support
132. New community status would have a range of advantages for local providers, principally funding (drawn from savings from overall budget reductions), dedicated support for innovation, and greater independence to innovate. But it would also give providers a range of appropriate challenges to drive their innovation activities, including money-saving targets and the responsibility to work with the social sector and their communities to develop new approaches. These advantages and challenges are described below.

133. In terms of funding, each year of the next spending review period a 'rebate' would be made available, equivalent to up to 1 per cent of the annual health, justice or social care budgets of participating providers, in return for a commitment to use this money to invest in innovation activities that seek to manage and reduce demand more effectively (and so prove cheaper) than existing approaches.

134. This funding would come with two commitments: providers would have to return half of the savings they make as a result of innovation activities to central government each year; and they would have to 'repay' at least half of the rebate to central government by the end of the Spending Review period.[99] This would in effect create a challenging target for the level of savings that would need to be produced from innovation efforts. Providers would have the right to retain and reinvest the other half of the savings from innovation as they wish.

135. In justice and social care, local authorities would be able to claim for a rebate in social work spending (which includes spending on community justice, CJSW, activities).[100] In health, local health boards would be able to claim for a rebate in local health spending, with a duty to work in partnership with local authorities and negotiate shared savings targets. Providers would decide how much they want to claim, up to the 1 per cent maximum per year (providers would of course be free to invest more of their own budgets if they wish, or to draw on

PART 3: TRANSFORMING SCOTLAND'S PUBLIC SERVICES 43

other sources of funding and support). Naturally there would be a difference in the size of the investment contingent on the size of the participating authority or public body.

136. As an illustration based on current spending, the average participating council would receive up to £1.1 million per year to invest in different approaches to justice and social work (a total of £4.4 million over the spending review period if the full amount was claimed each year) and would have to 're-pay' £2.2 million at the end of the period, plus half of all monies saved through innovation using this funding. If half of Scotland's local authorities claimed the full 1 per cent of the annual spend on total social work (including CJSW spending), this would amount to £70 million of total funds made available over the next four years (or £17.5 million per year).

137. As an equivalent in health, the average local health board would receive up to £5.3 million per year to invest in different approaches in health (a total of £21.2 million over four years if the full amount was claimed) and would have to repay £10.6 million in 2014-15, plus half of all monies saved. In total funds, this would amount to £148.4 million over the next four years (or £37.1 million per year).[101]

138. As noted above, this does not require additional net resources, since it would be funded through disinvestment in existing demand-led approaches and services. For example, in the course of the shift from containment to prevention and rehabilitation, a 10 per cent reduction in the costs of the prison system would suggest savings of £200 million during the next spending review period. Even if half of all councils claimed the maximum rebate for four straight years, this could still be financed by the reduction in spending in the prison service.

139. Alongside this funding, new community providers should receive dedicated support for their innovation activities from intermediary organisations. Engaging in radical innovation obviously requires some familiarity with useful strategies and tools, and a general ability to lead major change in organisations. This calls for a strengthened innovation support offer for local providers. This could for example be based on an approach that NESTA has developed with the Innovation Unit called 'radical efficiency', which has been used successfully with

a range of public service organisations.[102]

140. Part of the funding for this support would come from the additional resources available to providers through the rebate, but it is also likely that the Scottish Government would have to increase its investment in existing support agencies such as the Improvement Service while encouraging a greater focus on innovation alongside more traditional improvement activities.

Autonomy and responsibility

141. New community providers would be given greater freedoms from central audit, performance measurement and inspection. For local authorities and health boards, there would be far fewer obligations to report on centrally determined performance measures and targets.[103] For these providers, inspection and financial audit would take the form of a lighter-touch process of 'assurance' to ensure basic safety and probity.

142. In return, there would be a greater emphasis on locally-developed measures that are more appropriate to new approaches. Firstly, providers would be obliged to conduct a local 'total value' assessment of how and where resources are currently spent in their area of reform, and to identify and make public their targets for reducing that spending which is primarily demand-led.[104] Secondly, providers would be under a duty to develop their own performance indicators and long-term outcome-based measures of success, based on local priorities and the outcomes that local users of services want. (Providers would be able to request external evaluation if local indicators and/or user feedback suggest underlying, systemic problems in services.)

143. More generally, new community status would bring with it a general obligation to openness. Providers would be expected to share learning with other providers, central government, support organisations and the public. They should of course engage in on-going internal and external evaluation, but wherever appropriate make this publicly available. They should also open up their data to the public (including spending data, due to be published from April in line with Westminster Government commitments).

Social partnership and public participation

144. Finally, new community status would be based on a commitment to work in partnership with employees, the social sector, and the local community to develop and deliver new approaches. While an obligation, this emphasis on working in partnership should of course also be regarded by providers as an invaluable resource for innovation – for new ideas and for new collaborations to deliver these ideas in practice.

145. New community providers would make a commitment to work directly with frontline staff in designing and developing new approaches. We recognise that this will be made more difficult by the general context of budget reductions and staff losses, but organisations will have to do more to engage their employees in innovation, especially to empower middle management and frontline staff.[105] This should include supporting staff to explore alternative models of ownership for services (such as co-operatives, mutuals or social enterprises) and offering assistance for workers facing redundancy to create new organisations along these lines. The latter would be an important vehicle to capitalise on the skill and expertise of these employees, and would be especially effective where providers agree to support the development of these new enterprises by commissioning them to deliver services.

146. As might be expected, new community providers should also form partnerships with other relevant providers to develop and deliver innovative approaches. For example, a health board wishing to shift to more community provision would need to agree a partnership with the local authority, but since partnerships have already been formed we would expect these organisations to work through existing partnership arrangements rather than new mechanisms.

147. Providers would also make a commitment to work in new 'social partnerships' with a wider group of social enterprises, community groups and third sector organisations. This would help providers to identify, develop and deliver new approaches; it would also strengthen the local social sector and local communities.[106]

148. As part of this commitment, some providers might wish to establish small development funds for local social sector

organisations. NESTA's Big Green Challenge (which informed the Scottish Government's Low Carbon Community Challenge) demonstrates the significant impact that small amounts of money can have when used to support highly innovative social sector projects at an early stage.[107] As well as developing new approaches, such projects can help to build the capacity of communities to respond to local issues. One model for this is the establishing of a local 'community endowment' that can invest in enterprises which can develop their own sustainable revenues over time.

149. Providers should also ensure that the wider community is engaged in innovation. Many Scottish local authorities have established citizens' juries; these should be continued and expanded. In particular, providers could use participatory budgeting techniques to inform and shape their spending priorities. Involving the users of services and the public via such techniques can lead to an agreed focus on priorities, better decisions on reductions in spending, and also stimulate the public to develop their own approaches to meeting needs that have historically been met by the public sector.[108]

CONCLUSION

150. This paper suggests an approach to making sustainable savings in Scotland's public services that can help to meet the short-term challenges of the next few years and the long-term challenges of the future. If Scotland is to reduce spending without harming its economy and society, innovation in public services needs to play a much more significant role in the Scottish Government's strategy towards spending reductions – starting as soon as possible.

151. Over the past ten years, Scotland has introduced some important reforms to public services. It is now critical to focus reform on managing and reducing demand, through services which meet people's needs more effectively and build their own capability to prevent and respond to problems. The examples included in this paper demonstrate what can be achieved; the task now is to create the conditions to ensure that such approaches become the norm in Scotland's public services.

152. This kind of radical reform does not mean avoiding difficult decisions. If new approaches are to save money, they must enable reduced spending in some aspects of existing provision. But even in these difficult times, the opportunity also exists to introduce new approaches in public services which could help to ensure a stronger, safer, healthier and more productive Scotland.

ENDNOTES

1. Goudie, A. (2010) 'Outlook for Scottish Government Expenditure – June 2010 Emergency Budget Update.' Edinburgh: Office of the Chief Economic Adviser, Scottish Government.
2. Ibid.
3. These figures do not include other commitments such as pension liabilities, suggested as being £43-53 billion according to the Auditor General for Scotland, or the Scottish Government's estimate of the potential cost of commitments on climate change (£8 billion by 2022), both noted in the IBR. Projections for increasing costs in public services, for example due to an ageing population, are noted further below.
4. This is different from total public sector expenditure for Scotland, which includes spending on non-devolved areas, especially welfare payments and unemployment benefits. This total was estimated at £56.5 billion in 2008-09 (equivalent to 9.4 per cent of total UK public sector expenditure) when a share of the Westminster Government's financial sector interventions is included, or £55.8 billion (9.4 per cent of total UK public sector expenditure), when these are not included. See Scottish Government (2010) 'Government Expenditure and Revenue Scotland 2008-09.' Edinburgh: Scottish Government.
5. Beveridge, C.W. (2010) 'Independent Budget Review.' Edinburgh: Scotland's Independent Budget Review Panel.
6. However, as in the rest of the UK, Audit Scotland has stated that it is unable to assure the accuracy of the reported savings. See Audit Scotland (2010) 'Improving Public Sector Efficiency.' Edinburgh: Audit Scotland.
7. In 2008, the Scottish Government published its plans to reduce the total number of public bodies by 25 per cent by 2011. As a consequence of the Simplification Programme, the number of public bodies has been reduced from 199 to its current level of 160.
8. For example, according to the IBR, if the Scottish health budget (the health element of the Health and Wellbeing Portfolio) is protected and increases at the projected rate of inflation, the budget for non-health spending could decline by 10 per cent in real terms in 2011-12 and by 20 per cent by 2014-15, compared with 2010-11.
9. The IBR also discusses a number of options which it doesn't cost, including: reducing scrutiny and regulation; shared services; outsourcing; rationalising procurement; better absence management; reviewing free school meals; reviewing the graduate contribution to higher education and tuition fees; alternative financing methods for capital procurement; rationalising public assets; road user charging; changing pensions and employers' National Insurance contributions; and the potential saving from the abolition of Council Tax freeze (in the case of the latter, local authorities would likely be compensated by an increase in the local government settlement).

10. This calculation is based on the total money-saving measures costed in the IBR and their projected savings by 2014-15. These savings amount to £2,792 billion in total, around three-quarters of the required reductions in spending. Costed measures include: a one penny change in the Scottish variable rate (£1,600 million); achieving a higher 3 per cent efficiency target (£900 million); Simplification programme (£195 million); 'Option 1' on concessionary travel (£279 million); 'Option 1' on residential care (£279 million); a flat weekly fee of £77 for care at home clients (£647 million); 'Option 5' on prescription charges (£128 million); charges for NHS eye examinations for non-exempt categories of people (£93 million). Source: Independent Budget Review with NESTA calculations. This calculation also includes 'Option 1' on a pay decision for 2011-12 which amounts to £1.17 billion. This measure actually produces an additional 'funding gap'. If this were eliminated through redundancy for public sector workers, it would mean a reduction in headcount of 40,000 people. The overall pay bill would still increase under these options because: staff would still receive progression pay; under 'Option 1' 47 per cent of staff (those who are paid under £21,000) would be excluded from the pay freeze and would receive an increase of at least £250; and increases in employers' National Insurance and employers' pension contributions.

11. In 2008-09, the ratio of total managed expenditure (TME) for Scotland to GDP was 51.2 per cent excluding North Sea GDP and 49.9 per cent including a per capita share (41 per cent when an 'illustrative geographical share' of North Sea GDP is included). See Scottish Government (2010) 'Government Expenditure and Revenue Scotland 2008-09.' Edinburgh: Scottish Government.

12. In the first quarter of 2010 there were 573,900 people employed in the public sector in Scotland (506,000 in devolved public bodies), representing 23.6 per cent of total employment. This is higher than the UK average of 19.8 per cent but below that in Northern Ireland (28.8 per cent). See Scottish Government/National Statistics (2010) 'Public Sector Employment in Scotland: Statistics for 1st Quarter 2010.' Edinburgh/Newport: Scottish Government/National Statistics.

13. According to one analysis, the public sector has contributed to over 30 per cent of Scotland's GDP growth over the last ten years, compared to just 20 per cent in the rest of the UK. See Ernst & Young Scottish Item Club (2010) 'Economic Prospects 2010.' London: Ernst & Young Scottish Item Club. One estimate suggests that spending reductions could result in up to 126,000 job losses across the Scottish economy by 2014-15 (comprising up to 90,000 public sector and 37,000 private sector jobs). See Fraser of Allander Institute (2010) 'Economic Commentary.' Vol.34, No.1, June. However, when flexibility in prices (especially wages) is allowed, the impact on job losses in the public sector is much smaller at 78,000 and private sector employment could rise by 14,000. In terms of direct job losses, the IBR estimates that in order to close the gap in the pay bill budget, public sector employment would need to fall by approximately 5.7 per cent to 10 per cent (between 35,000 and 60,000 public sector jobs) by 2014-15 (depending on the pay restraint options selected). This assumes a pay freeze in the first two years and pay restraint in the following two years.

14. However, even in this area improvement has started to plateau and Scotland remains a distance from its target to ending child poverty by 2020. See Sinclair, S. and McKendrick, J. (2009) 'Child Poverty in Scotland: taking the next steps.' York: Joseph Rowntree Foundation.

15. For example, an influential Joseph Rowntree report showed the consequences of child poverty to be wide-ranging and long-lasting with subsequent costs to a range of services such as education, health and criminal justice. See Hirsh, D. (2008) 'Estimating the Costs of Child Poverty: round-up.' York: Joseph Rowntree Foundation.

16. Department for Work and Pension's Family Resources Survey, Households Below Average Income datasets.

17. Parekh, A. (2010) 'Monitoring Poverty and Social Exclusion in Scotland 2010.' York: Joseph Rowntree Foundation.

18. Identifiable expenditure only. See Scottish Government (2010) 'Government Expenditure and Revenue Scotland 2008-09.' Edinburgh: Scottish Government. There are a number of reasons why per capita expenditure is typically greater in Scotland compared to the UK as a whole, including: the importance of particular activities for Scotland (for example agriculture, fisheries and forestry); Scotland's lower population

ENDNOTES

density which increases the cost of providing the same level of provision; the scope and remit of the public sector in Scotland compared to the UK (for example water and sewage services are a public sector responsibility in Scotland whereas in England they are operated by the private sector); and greater demand for provision in Scotland (for example, in higher education, health and housing).

19. Health Scotland (2010) 'Fresh Air? Second Hand Smoke: an overview of the main outcomes of the evaluation of the smoke-free legislation.' Edinburgh: Health Scotland.

20. The years to which the data relates reflect the typical time lag in compiling international comparative statistics.

21. Ischaemic or ischemic heart disease (IHD), or myocardial ischaemia, is a disease characterised by ischaemia (reduced blood supply) to the heart muscle, usually due to coronary artery disease (atherosclerosis of the coronary arteries). Its risk increases with age, smoking, hypercholesterolaemia (high cholesterol levels), diabetes, and hypertension (high blood pressure).

22. Audit Scotland uses a fairly wide definition of 'long-term conditions' in this estimate so may account for a larger proportion of the population. See Audit Scotland (2007) 'Managing Long-term Conditions.' Edinburgh: Audit Scotland.

23. NHS Quality and Improvement Service (2007) 'Management of Coronary Heart Disease: a clinical and resource impact assessment.' Edinburgh: NHS Scotland.

24. Bloor, M., Gannon, M., Hay, G., Jackson, G., Leyland, A. and McKeganey, N. (2008) Contribution of problem drug users' deaths to excess mortality in Scotland: Secondary analysis of cohort study. 'British Medical Journal.' 337:a478.

25. UK data for long term conditions drawn from Foresight/Government Office for Science (2007) 'Tackling Obesities: Future Choices – Modelling Future Trends in Obesity and Their Impact on Health.' 2nd Edition. London: Foresight/Government Office for Science. Figures quoted are the total cost of long-term conditions to the NHS, not just those conditions attributable to elevated BMI (overweight and obesity). Data adjusted for Scotland on the basis of population size; this probably understates the costs of these conditions in Scotland, given their greater prevalence in Scotland.

26. Glennerster, H. (2010) 'Financing the UK's Welfare States.' London: 2020 Public Services Trust at the RSA.

27. Scotland and European Health for All (HfA) Database 2009.

28. Scottish Government, COSLA, NHS Scotland (2010) 'Reshaping Care for Older People, Information Booklet.' Edinburgh: Scottish Government.

29. Ibid.

30. Ibid.

31. Scottish Government (2010) 'High Level Summary of Statistics, Crime and Justice.' Edinburgh: Scottish Government; also Muir, R. (2010) Crime and Justice after Devolution. In Lodge, G. and Schmuecker, K. (Eds) 'Devolution in Practice 2010.' London: IPPR.

32. Scottish Consortium on Crime and Criminal Justice (2010) 'Crime and Justice in Scotland 2009: A fourth review of progress.' Edinburgh: Scottish Consortium on Crime and Criminal Justice.

33. Scottish Prison Service (2010) 'Delivery Plan 2010/11.' Edinburgh: Scottish Prison Service.

34. Scottish Government (2010) 'Scottish Prison Population Projections: 2009-10 to 2018-19.' Edinburgh: Scottish Government.

35. Spencer, A. (2007) 'The Cost Of Unnecessary Imprisonment.' Glasgow: Scottish Consortium on Crime and Criminal Justice.

36. Scottish Consortium on Crime and Criminal Justice (2010) 'Crime and Justice in Scotland 2009: A Fourth Review of Progress.' Edinburgh: Scottish Consortium on Crime and Criminal Justice.

37. Houchin, R. (2005) 'Social Exclusion and Imprisonment in Scotland: A Report.' Glasgow: Glasgow Caledonian University.

ENDNOTES

38. The Scottish Household Survey suggests that 64.9 per cent of adults were satisfied with local health services, local schools and public transport in 2009. See Scottish Government/National Statistics (2009) 'Scottish Household Survey 2009.' Edinburgh/Newport: Scottish Government/National Statistics.
39. Lodge, G. and Schmuecker, K. (Eds) (2010) 'Devolution in Practice 2010.' London: IPPR.
40. In November 2007 the Scottish Government and the Convention of Scottish Local Authorities (COSLA) signed a concordat, which committed both to moving towards Single Outcome Agreements (SOAs) for all 32 of Scotland's councils and extending these to Community Planning Partnerships (CPPs). SOAs are agreements which set out how each party will work towards improving outcomes for local people in a way that reflects local circumstances and priorities, but within the context of the Government's National Outcomes.
41. 2020 Public Services Trust at the RSA (2009) 'A Brief History of Public Service Reform.' London: RSA.
42. Dixon, A. (2007) 'Engaging Patients in their Health: How the NHS Needs to Change.' London: The King's Fund; also Hannah, M. (2010) 'Costing an Arm and a Leg.' Edinburgh: International Futures Forum; also Wanless, D. (2002) The Health Service in 2022. In Department of Health (2002) 'Securing our Future Health.' London: Department of Health.
43. The OECD notes that long-term demographic shifts and health care trends mean that between now and 2050, public spending on health and long-term care could almost double as a share of GDP in the average OECD country in the absence of policy action to break with past trends in this area. See OECD (2006) 'Projecting OECD Health and Long-term Care Expenditures: What are the main drivers?' Paris: OECD.
44. Sassi, F. and Hurst, J. (2008) 'The Prevention of Lifestyle-Related Chronic Diseases: Economic Framework.' OECD Health Working Paper No.32. Paris: OECD.
45. Bunt, L. and Harris, M. (2009) 'The Human Factor.' NESTA: London.
46. Scottish Government (2007) 'Better Health, Better Care: Action Plan.' Edinburgh: Scottish Government.
47. Scottish Government (2009) 'Towards a Mentally Flourishing Scotland: Action Plan 2009-2011.' Edinburgh: Scottish Government.
48. Kerr, D. (2005) 'Building a Health Service Fit for the Future.' Edinburgh: Scottish Executive. There are currently a small number of test sites trialling an integrated approach to financing health and social care. The Integrated Resource Framework, developed jointly by the Scottish Government, NHS Scotland and the Convention of Scottish Local Authorities (COSLA), is designed to develop a better model for the better use of resources across and within health and adult social care services.
49. Health England (2009) Prevention and Preventative Spending. In Social Finance (2009) 'Social Impact Bands: Rethinking Finance for Social Outcomes.' London: Social Finance Ltd.
50. Joy, I. and Miller, I. (2006) 'Don't Mind Me: Adult Mental Health Problems.' London: New Philanthropy Capital.
51. Puska, P. (2002) 'The North Karelia Project: Pioneering Work to Improve National Public Health.' Helsinki: National Public Health Institute.
52. Ibid.
53. For example, the 'Hartslag Limburg' ('Heartbeat Limburg') from the Netherlands drew on the interdisciplinary approach in North Karelia to design a multi-faceted strategy to reduce CVD in the Limburg region and the 10,000 Steps project from Queensland Australia, promoting physical activity through social networks and community-based campaigns. See Ronckers, E.T., Groot, W., Steenbakkers, M., Ruland, E., et al. (2006) Costs of the Hartslag Limburg Community Heart Health Intervention. 'BMC Public Health.' 6, 51.
54. See Puska, P. (2002) Successful Prevention of Non-Communicable Diseases: 25 years with North Karelia Project in Finland. 'Public Health Medicine.' 4 (1), pp.5-7; also Shea, S. and Basch, C.E. (1990) A Review of Five Major Community-based Cardiovascular

ENDNOTES

Disease Prevention Programmes. 'American Journal of Health Promotion.' 4 (4), pp.279-87.

55. Scottish Government (2010) 'Preventing Overweight and Obesity in Scotland: a routemap towards healthy weight.' Edinburgh: Scottish Government.

56. Scottish Government (2008) 'Healthy Eating, Active Living: An Action Plan to Improve Diet, Increase Physical Activity and Tackle Obesity, 2008-2011.' Edinburgh: Scottish Government.

57. The Equally Well Test Sites were introduced following the recommendation from the Equally Well Task Force on Health Inequalities in Scotland. See Scottish Government (2008) 'Equally Well: report of the Ministerial Task Force on Health Inequalities.' Edinburgh: Scottish Government.

58. Rural Policy Centre (2010) 'Rural Scotland in Focus 2010.' Edinburgh: Rural Policy Centre.

59. Scottish Government (2008) 'The Road to Recovery: A New Approach to Tackling Scotland's Drug Problem.' Edinburgh: Scottish Government.

60. Audit Scotland estimates these costs as follows: £2.734 billion to the criminal justice system from drug and alcohol-related crime; £488 million to NHS Scotland in hospital admissions; £182 million for social services; £626 million in 'social/human costs'; and £820 million in economic costs from unemployment, workplace absence and lost productivity. See Audit Scotland (2008) 'Drug and Alcohol Services in Scotland.' Edinburgh: Audit Scotland.

61. Scottish Government (2008) 'The Road to Recovery: A New Approach to Tackling Scotland's Drug Problem.' Edinburgh: Scottish Government.

62. The Sunrise Project was funded and evaluated by the Big Lottery Fund 'Better-Off' programme. See Big Lottery Fund (2008) 'Better-Off Evaluation: Final report.' Edinburgh: Big Lottery Fund.

63. The programme has received funding from the Fairer Scotland Fund, targeted at deprived communities and devolved to local authority spending as part of Single Outcome Agreements. See Fairer Scotland Fund (2010) 'Annual Report 2009-2010.' Edinburgh: Fairer Scotland Fund.

64. See RSA Projects, User Centred Drug Services. Available at: www.thersa.org/projects/user-centred-drug-services

65. Audit Scotland (2008) 'Drug and Alcohol Services in Scotland.' Edinburgh: Audit Scotland.

66. Jeffery, C. (2009) 'Older People, Public Policy and the Impact of Devolution in Scotland.' Edinburgh: Age Scotland.

67. Boyle, D. and Harris, M. (2009) 'The Challenge of Co-production.' London: NESTA.

68. Scottish Government (2010) 'Reshaping Care for Older People Programme, Information Booklet.' Edinburgh: Scottish Government.

69. Wanless, D. (2006) 'Securing Good Care for Older People: Taking a Long-term View.' London: The King's Fund.

70. Scottish Government (2008) 'Guidance for Local Authorities and Health Boards on the Implementation of Local Area Coordination for People with Learning Disabilities.' Edinburgh: Scottish Government; also Bartnik, E. et al. (2003) 'Review of the Local Area Co-ordination Program Western Australia.' Perth: Government of Western Australia and Disability Services Commission.

71. Scotland's Future Forum (2010) 'Report to the Scottish Parliament's Finance Committee Inquiry: Funding for Public Services.' Edinburgh: Scotland's Future Forum. Calculations based upon work undertaken by Price Waterhouse Coopers (PWC), pp.5. See also Fitzpatrick, J. (2006) Dreaming for Real: the development of Partners for Inclusion. 'Journal of Integrated Care.' 14 (1), February.

72. University of Stirling (2005) 'Smart Technology and Community Care for Older People: Innovation in West Lothian, Scotland.' Edinburgh: Age Concern Scotland.

ENDNOTES

73. Boyle, D., Slay, J. and Stephens, L. (2010) 'Public Services Inside Out: Putting Co-production into Practice.' London: NESTA and nef.
74. According to one analysis, a more effective approach to preventing recidivism amongst the most prolific offender group could reduce the costs of the criminal justice system by around £1 billion a year. See Mulheirn, I., Gough, B. and Menne, V. (2010) 'Prison Break: Tackling Recidivism, Reducing Costs.' London: Social Market Foundation.
75. Home Office (2010) 'Cutting Crime: The Case for Justice Reinvestment.' London: Home Office.
76. The Scottish Prisons Commission (2008) 'Scotland's Choice, Report of the Scottish Prisons Commission.' Edinburgh: The Scottish Prisons Commission.
77. Scottish Parliament (2010) 'Criminal Justice and Licensing (Scotland) Bill.' Edinburgh: Scottish Parliament.
78. Scottish Executive (2006) 'The National Strategy for the Management of Offenders.' Edinburgh: Scottish Executive; also Audit Scotland (2008) 'Managing Increasing Prisoner Numbers in Scotland.' Edinburgh: Audit Scotland.
79. House of Commons Justice Committee (2010) 'Cutting Crime: The Case for Justice Reinvestment.' London: The Stationery Office.
80. Ross, H. (2008) 'Justice Reinvestment: What it is and why it may be an idea to consider in Scotland.' Edinburgh: CjScotland.
81. Hurley, N., Dorrans, S., Orr, D. and Eaves, J. (2008) 'Evaluation of School, Social Work, Police and Community Project: East Renfrewshire Council, East Renfrewshire CHCP.' Edinburgh: Blake Stevenson Research.
82. Restorative Justice Consortium (2009) 'Summary of Ministry of Justice Research into Restorative Justice.' London: Restorative Justice Consortium.
83. Home Office (2004) 'Reoffending of Adults: Results from 2004 Cohort.' London: Home Office. See also Social Finance (2009) 'Social Impact Bonds: Rethinking Finance for Social Outcomes.' London: Social Finance.
84. Centre for Social Justice (2008) 'Breakthrough Glasgow: Ending the Costs of Social Breakdown.' London: Centre for Social Justice; also Hanlon, P., Walsh, D. and Whyte, B. (2006) 'Let Glasgow Flourish.' Glasgow: Glasgow Centre for Population Health.
85. Centre for Social Justice (2008) 'Breakthrough Glasgow.' London: Centre for Social Justice.
86. Ibid.
87. Violence Reduction Unit (2010) 'Community Initiative to Reduce Violence: Third Quarter Progress Report.' Glasgow: Violence Reduction Unit.
88. Scottish Government (2010) 'Scotland's Budget Documents 2010-11: Budget (Scotland) Bill Supporting Document for the year ending 31 March 2011.' Edinburgh: Scottish Government.
89. Howie, M. (2008) Knife crime cut by fifth thanks to youth crackdown...Danish style. 'The Scotsman.' 23rd July.
90. Scottish Government (2008) 'Equally Well: Report of the Ministerial Task Force on Health Inequalities.' Edinburgh: Scottish Government.
91. In the wake of the Crerar Review in 2007, the Scottish Government's intention is to shift responsibility for scrutiny towards service deliverers themselves to drive forward improvement through a greater emphasis on self-assessment and reporting. Good progress has been made to reduce the burden of external scrutiny since the publication of the Crerar Review including reducing the number of scrutiny bodies to 29, a reduction of seven compared with three years ago.
92. Bartnik, E. *et al.* (2003) 'Review of the Local Area Co-ordination Program Western Australia.' Perth: Government of Western Australia and Disability Services Commission.
93. Sir John Arbuthnott's report on the potential for shared services across eight councils in the Clyde Valley identified a number of ways that councils could work together to respond to local priorities, in particular through integrating health and social care services.

ENDNOTES

94. The 'social sector' includes the voluntary sector, which is sizeable in Scotland. There are around 45,000 voluntary organisations, about half of which are registered charities. The sector manages an income of around £4.4 billion a year. The voluntary sector is a major provider of public services, particularly to local government and the health service as well as substantial provision of social care, rehabilitation services for drug and alcohol users and employment initiatives. See SCVO (2010) 'Submission from the Scottish Council for Voluntary Organisations to the Finance Committee Inquiry into Preventative Spending.' Edinburgh: SCVO.

95. This 'disinvestment/re-investment' approach was also a recommendation by the Convention for Scottish Local Authorities (COSLA) in their submission to the Scottish Government's Finance Committee Inquiry on Preventative Spending. See COSLA (2010) 'Inquiry into Preventative Spending: Submission from COSLA.' Edinburgh: COSLA.

96. One model is provided by the West Lothian Impact Assessment.

97. This recommendation builds on a report based on work conducted for NESTA by the Innovation Unit. See Gillinson, S., Horne, M. and Baeck, P. (2010) 'Radical Efficiency.' NESTA: London.

98. This would mean that the current Concordat between the Scottish Government and Scottish local authorities would have to be renewed in some form for the next Spending Review period.

99. It seems sensible that the 'repayment' would be easiest to administer in the form of a budget allocation for the local provider reduced by the amount of the money to be reallocated to central government – in other words, the amount would just be taken off the next budget allocation.

100. Local authorities plan and monitor offender management and provide community justice services through Community Justice Authorities (CJAs), the statutory bodies created by the Management of Offenders etc. (Scotland) Act 2005. Community Justice Authorities are made up of the local authority (represented by some of the elected members), with attendance from other statutory partners who work with offenders locally, such as social work departments, the Scottish Prison Service (SPS), Police, the Procurator Fiscal, Victim Support Scotland.

101. These calculations are estimates based on current local authority and health board budgets, drawn primarily from Audit Scotland (2010) 'An Overview of Local Government in Scotland 2009.' Edinburgh: Audit Scotland; and Scottish Government details on funding for NHS Boards.

102. See Gillinson, S., Horne, M. and Baeck, P. (2010) 'Radical Efficiency.' NESTA: London.

103. Currently, local authorities have to report on the Statutory Performance Indicators set by the Accounts Commission for Scotland, while health boards have to report on the national HEAT targets agreed with the Scottish Government.

104. This builds on the Total Place programme that has been piloted in England, but focusing more on the value (impact) produced by spending (as suggested by John Seddon in his critique of Total Place). See Seddon, J. (2009) 'Total Place, A Proposal to Employ an Alternative Method to Achieve the Aims of Total Place.' Buckingham: Vanguard Consulting.

105. Patterson, F., Kerrin, M., Gatto-Roissard, G. and Coan, P. (2009) 'Everyday Innovation: How to Enhance Innovative Working in Employees and Organisations.' London: NESTA.

106. See for example the guidance developed by the National Audit Office for commissioning third sector groups. Available at: www.nao.org.uk/guidance_and_good_practice/toolkits/successful_commissioning.aspx

107. Bunt, L. and Harris, M. (2010) 'Mass Localism.' London: NESTA.

108. See for example IPSOS Mori/Leicestershire County Council (2010) 'Leicestershire County Council Budget Consultation 2010/11, Full report.' London/Leicester: IPSOS Mori/Leicestershire County Council; also Wood, T. and Murray, W.E. (2007) Participatory Democracy in Brazil and Local Geographies: Porto Alegre and Belo Horizonte Compared. 'European Review of Latin American and Caribbean Studies.' 83, October, pp.19-41.